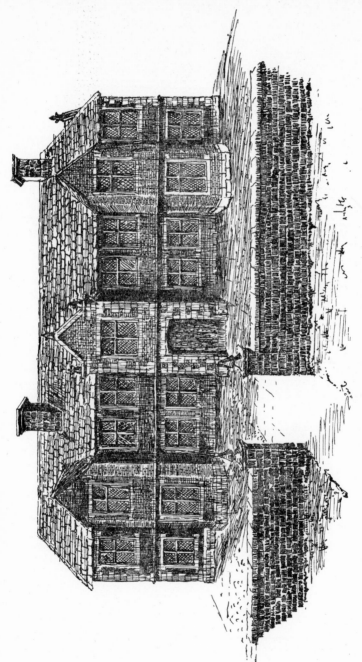

CLARKE HALL IN 1712

CLARKE HALL
its Builders and Owners
by
H. C. Haldane, F.S.A.

Published by the Wakefield Historical Society
1957

CLARKE HALL

Two hundred and fifty copies of this book have
been printed

This copy is number ....**218**.............

Signed .....*H C Haldane*.....................

PREFACE

" It is a reverend thing to see an ancient castle or building not in decay, or to see a fair timber tree sound and perfect; how much more to behold an ancient family, which hath stood against the wares and weathers of time."

Thus wrote Bacon which is particularly suited to this old hall and its builders.

My intention has been to put on record all that I have been able to gather concerning the house and its occupants, lest in time to come and the march of progress all might be swept away in this materialistic age under the guise of civic progress, which is often but another name for vandalism in the highest places and cloaked by the name of Town Planning improvements.

Having seen the fate of such fine old houses as Alverthorpe Hall, Haselden Hall, Chevet Hall, Flanshaw Hall and Bretton Hall Stables, I decided to place on record as much as possible concerning this building and its inhabitants in the hope that it may continue to survive and serve a useful purpose as long as possible, and the book may influence the rising generation to pause before they ruthlessly sweep away worthwhile buildings which may have many years of service in their massive walls and timbers and replace them with garish and shoddy erections.

Do take care of Kettlethorpe Hall and Lupset Hall, which latter has descended to be a golf club.

I am very grateful to the Misses Walker for permission to use the Bradford and Wingfield and Clarke pedigrees from Dr. Walker's " History of Wakefield " and other extracts. Also for his account of the 2nd Battle of Wakefield on Whit Sunday, May 21st, 1643, which he was able to compile from the Public Records in the House of Lords library after I had brought to his notice the field names from the estate plans of the Cannonry,

Great Gun Croft and the Little Gun Croft: Also to Captain Alexander Haldane, of Gleneagles, the present laird [27], for permission to show an illustration of Gleneagles House and also of the portrait of John Haldane, the then laird at the time of the 1715 Rebellion, who was M.P. for Perthshire; to Mr. F. Grundy for his great help with plans dealing with St. Swithun's Chapel: to Mr. H. Speak, the Secretary of the Wakefield Historical Society, for his great help in dealing with the applications for and distribution of volumes to the subscribers for the book and finally to the Wakefield Express Series, Ltd., for great care they have taken in the printing of the book and their Press notices.

DEDICATION

I dedicate this book to my wife as an appreciation of all the loyalty she has given me in my restoration of the old home and the preservation of all its old features. That meant much forbearance in living in a house whilst it was being upset in the removal of undesirable features of the 19th Century and opening out the large number of windows which had been walled up in the past to escape window tax, 19 in all.

THE Village Green of Stanley formerly extended from Bar Lane near the Old Toll Bar to the grounds of the West Riding Asylum, covering an area of about 7½ acres, with the turnpike road to Aberford and York running through the middle. It was surrounded by the grounds of four important houses: Colley Hall on its south east side, in a field still bearing the name of Colley Hall field; Bradford Hall on the east side, but now known as Clarke Hall; Midgeley Hall on the north side but now called Stanley Hall; and lastly, Box or Vaux Hall on the north west side, but now only known by its field name.

BOX OR VAUX HALL

This stood at the north west corner of the Green between the site of the old Toll Bar and Field Head in the field marked Box Hall Croft on the map.

John Box lived there in 1512 and owned 12 acres of land in Ouchthorpe, Stanley, worth 13/- per ann. During the 17th Century the house and land had passed into the hands of a branch of the Maude family.

Since the middle of the 19th Century the whole of the portion west of the turnpike road has been enclosed in the Mental Hospital Board's grounds.

BRADFORD HALL NOW CLARKE HALL

The family of Bradford settled in the Wakefield district early in the fifteenth century and evidently came from the Bradford district, judging from the amount of property they already possessed in that area and mentioned in their several wills.

The earliest members of the family at Stanley were Thomas, clerk, and William, also of Heath, to whom at a Manor Great Court held in October, 1436, " John Frankyske, late of Stanley, surrendered ½ acre in Helliefield." Also in the same year John Staneley, of Stanley, surrendered 6 acres in Stanley to Thos. Bradford, clerk. In the next year, 1437, there was a suit between John Lake, William Bradford and Thomas Beaumont,

complainants, and John Stanley, late of Stanley, and
Joan, his wife, deforciants of one messuage and 2 acres
of meadow with appurtenances — the right of W.
Bradford.*

This is the first purchase of a house in Stanley by
the Bradfords. Probably this house would be the
original building which stood on the site of the present
structure, remains of which I have come across from
time to time, e.g., foundations of wall underneath the
present rooms, and also continuing outside into the
garden and the forecourt.

William Bradford paid a heriot to the Lord of the
Manor on May 22nd, 1472, as heir-at-law to his
brother, Thomas Bradford, Clerk, for 8 acres of land in
Stanley, and at the same court surrendered the same
8 acres to his son Brian, the first of that name, who was
an attorney-at-law. By his will proven January 23rd,
1476, Wm. Bradford left his lands in Stanley, Ouchthorpe, and Wakefield to his son, Brian, who took up
residence in the old house which had also a cobbled
pavement and channels 2 ft. below the present cobbled
courtyard.

In 1462, William Watson surrendered to Brian [1]
Bradford 1¾ acres of land lying upon the West Riddings.

In 1474, William Bradford of Heath made his will
and ordered that out of his lands in Purston Jacklin,
Featherstone and Ackton, a chaplain be found for seven
years, three of which to be at Warmfield and four years
at the Chapel of the Holy Trinity and St. Sithe at Ivy
Bridge in Bradford to say masses for the soul of the
testator, etc., etc.

To Isabel, his wife, he left his lands in le Heth and
Over Walton for her life.

To his son, Brian [1], his lands at Stanley, Ouchthorpe and Wakefield.

For the making of the bells at Warmfield 100/-.

*Fines of Henry 6th, 1437-28.

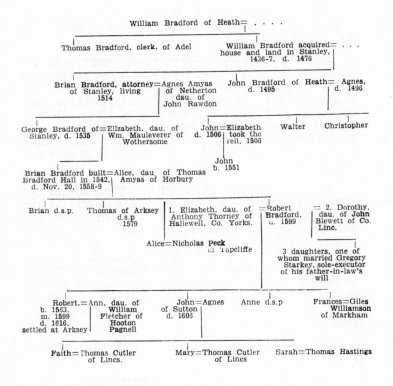

William Bradford of Heath= . . . .

Thomas Bradford, clerk, of Adel   William Bradford acquired= . . .
house and land in Stanley,
1436-7, d. 1476

Brian Bradford, attorney=Agnes Amyas   John Bradford of Heath= Agnes,
of Stanley, living   of Netherton   d. 1495   d. 1496
1514   dau. of
John Rawdon

George Bradford of=Elizabeth, dau. of   John=Elizabeth   Walter   Christopher
Stanley, d. 1535   Wm. Mauleverer of   d. 1506 took the
Wothersome   veil, 1506

John
b. 1551

Brian Bradford built=Alice, dau. of Thomas
Bradford Hall in 1542, Amyas of Horbury
d. Nov. 20, 1558-9

Brian d.s.p.   Thomas of Arksey   1. Elizabeth, dau. of   =Robert   == 2. Dorothy,
d.s.p   Anthony Thorney of   Bradford.   dau. of John
1579   Hallewell, Co. Yorks.   d. 1599   Blewett of Co.
Linc.

Alice=Nicholas Peck
of Topcliffe

3 daughters, one of
whom married Gregory
Starkey, sole-executor
of his father-in-law's
will

Robert.=Ann, dau. of   John=Agnes   Anne d.s.p   Frances=Giles
b. 1563,   William   of Sutton   Williamson
m. 1599   Fletcher of   d. 1606   of Markham
d. 1616,   Hooton
settled at Arksey   Pagnell

Faith=Thomas Cutler   Mary=Thomas Cutler   Sarah=Thomas Hastings
of Lincs.   of Lincs

To George Bradford, son of the above Brian Bradford, his best standing piece of silver and gold.

To his son, John Bradford, and Constance, his daughter, silver goblet together with the Heath, Warmfield, Sharlston and Bradford estates.

With the above Brian [1] Bradford, the line of Bradfords in Stanley begins. He was reeve of Stanley in 1492-3 and again in 1496-8.

In 1523, Brian [1] Bradford's name appears in the Subsidy Roll granted to Henry VIII for the carrying on of the War with France. He was rated at 6/8d. for 10 March lands. He was charged for his lands towards the Relief of Berwick on March 20th, 1564. He was ordered to be furnished with 1 Corselet and pyke, 1 harquebus and 1 morian or salade, 1 bow and a sheaf of arrows and 1 steel cap. The Place of Muster was Agbrigg Moor.*

In 1514, Brian [1] Bradford was fined 4d. for not appearing at a Manor Court. He was one of the Wardens of Wakefield Church in 1491. In 1492 he was elected Grave for Stanley, which office he again held in 1496 . In 1544 at the Lord's Court of the Manor it was reported that he had built and occupied one messuage and 12 acres of land with appurtenances in Stanley Graveship for the space of two years and more without paying the usual fine to the Lord (Wakefield Court Rolls) and so we get the date of the building on the present house 1542

Brian's son, George, died in his father's lifetime in 1535.

In 1546, Brian [1] Bradford, of Bradford Hall, Stanley, gentleman, made his will " giving his soul to God and his body to be buried in St. Nicholas Choir in the Parish Church of Wakefield as nigh unto his stall there as conveniently may be."

*Subsidy Rolls of Henry 8th.

In 1558, Brian (2) Bradford died and was buried also in St. Nicholas Choir of the Parish Church of Wakefield:—*

item He bequethed towards the amending and repairing of the hye waies about Stanley which are moste noysome 40/-.

item To the poor people in the town of Wakefield, £5.

item To the poor people in Stanley, Ouchthorpe, Newton, Wrenthorpe, Alverthorpe and Thornes 40/-.

item to the poor people in Horbury, 13/4d.

item I give and bequethe to the Parish Church of Wakefield one great chalice double gilt with the paten belonging and such copes, vestments and other ornaments as I have remaining in the said church for the maintenance of good services there as long as the lawes of this relm of England will permit and suffer the same to be so used.   And failing this, to my son, Robert Bradford.

item I give and bequethe unto Robert Bradford, my sonne, immediately after the death of my wife, Alice, one brewing lead in the kitchen, one standing table in the hall, one syde table and the cupboard in the said hall, one greate brasse potte, which was my grandfathers, one silver salte with a cover double gilte, one standing piece with a cover double gilte, one golde ringe which was my mothers, two silver spoones, and also all of my waynes, plowes, harrowes, and all other things p'teyning to husbandrye, etc.

Also I will that Robert Bradford, my sonne, shall have and enjoy the office and kepshippe of the Outwood of Wakefield with the fees and profites pertaining to the same so that he the said Robert does not put forthe Richard Swaynson from his service there upon his honstee and trew demenor.

Robert Bradford having suceeded his father, Brian (2), in 1558 when he was 30 years old he herioted for the estate on October 29th, 1559, at the Manor Court.*

In 1559 at an inquisition post mortem held at Wetherby on April 8th, 1559, before Mathew Wentworth, Esq., it was stated that Brian Bradford, formerly of Stanley, gentleman, died seized of a capital messuage called Stanley Hall, 20 acres of arable land, 20 acres of meadow and 20 acres of pasture in Stanley held in free soccage at 20/- rent and of the annual value of £5.   Also one tenement called Le Cliff in Wakefield worth 40/- per annum; also a close in Stanley called "Parsons Flat" containing about 18 acres; also a close worth 28/- per annum and 2 closes in Thornes worth 20/- per annum.

*Testamenta Leodiensis XXVII 256-8.

In 1563, 64, 68, 69, 70 and 72, Robert Bradford was the Grave of Stanley and in 1572 his name appears in the list of Minor Gentry of the West Riding prepared by Sir Thos. Gargrave for Lord Burghley, and there is shown as a protestant. On the painted frieze above the panelling in the Great Chamber at Gilling Castle, the Bradford shield of arms hangs amongst those of the Wapentake of Agbrigg.

In 1591 his estate was assessed at £13 6s. 8d. on which he paid a fine of 17/6d. per annum. He was also a Treasurer for Lame Soldiers.

In 1584 he entered his name and arms at the visitation held by Robert Glover and showed the following:—

quartley 1 and 4 Argent. A wolf's head proper erased between 3 bugle horns sable for Bradford: 2 and 3 Argent on a bend sable 3 roses of the field for Amyas. Crest a peacock's head proper in its beak and twined round its neck a serpent arg.

He was one of the first Governors of Queen Elizabeth Grammar School at Wakefield to which he contributed 10/- a year of his lands at Stanley.

At the low end of the street called the Springs, formerly stood an old hostelry called the " Bradford Arms " where now stands Mr. Stageman's shop. Probably it would be kept by an old retainer and used by the Bradfords to stable their horses when they drove into Wakefield for church services or for business.

In 1596-7 he was Grave of Stanley and died in 1599.

His eldest son, Robert, having heired his Uncle Thomas's property at Arksey where he went to live and married Ann Fletcher, of Hooten Paganel, the Stanley estates passed to his second son, John, as follows:—

" To my son, John, all the seilings, glass, lead and brewing vessels, bordes, tables, forms, iron ranges and cupboards which are being and remaining about my house at Stanley aforesaid, etc." The term seiling applied to loose sheets of boarding which were used as underdrawing for bedroom " comfort " against draught and snow from the slated roofs.

John Bradford did not long reside at Stanley, but removed to Sutton, near Brotherton, where he died in 1606.   By his will he left all his lands and property in Stanley to his three daughters:—

Faith, married to Thomas Cutler.

Mary, married to another Thomas Cutler.

Sara, married to Thomas Hastings.

This eventually caused the estate to be sold in order to have a division.   The purchaser in 1626 was Humphrey Wingfield, who married Priscilla Fleming, of Wakefield.

The Wingfields were descended from Sir Humphrey Wingfield, of Brantham Hall, in Suffolk, who was speaker in the House of Commons in 24 Henry VIII.

Humphrey Wingfield and his wife, Priscilla, had three daughters, Margaret, Mary and Elizabeth, who died unmarried, and also a son, Ferdinando, who was baptized in Wakefield in 1626 and later married Margaret, sister of John Storrie, of Hazleborrow, the benefactor to Wakefield Grammar School, who left all his property in the County of York to his sister for life and after her decease to maintain three poor boys at Oxford or Cambridge for three years.   He also gave £1,000 to his niece, Margaret Wingfield, if she married with her mother's consent and approbation, otherwise the money was to be used to educate three more poor boys at Oxford or Cambridge for three years.

The Hearth Tax was introduced in 1662.   Each hearth in houses of over £20 rateable value was taxed at 2/- per annum.

In Stanley Parish the following were taxable in 1672:—

Robert Benson, of Wrenthorpe Hall on 12 hearths.

Thomas Savile, of Lupset Park on 10 hearths.

1. Humphrey Wingfield=Priscilla, dau. of John　=2. John Lyon, M.D., of Stanley,
　of Bradford Hall,　　Fleming of Wakefield　　　bur. Oct. 24, 1631
　bur. Mar. 26, 1628　　by Elizabeth Roe,
　　　　　　　　　　　his wife
　　　　　　　　　　mar. Aug. 15, 1618

Ferdinando Wingfield=Margaret Storie, sister　=2nd husband,　　　　　Margaret
of Bradford Hall, bap.　and heir of John Storie　Thomas Conney of Leeds　Mary
May 27, 1621, bur. at　of Hasleborrow, the　　　　　　　　　　　　Elizabeth
Wakefield, June 30,　benefactor to the
　　1660　　　　　　Grammar School,
　　　　　　　　　bur. Mar. 26, 1687

Ferdinando　　Priscilla Wingfield,=Benjamin Clarke,　John Wingfield=Mary, dau. of
bap. Dec. 14,　bap. Oct. 21,　　of Hansworth,　　　of　　　　Richard
　1656,　　　　1648　　　　bought　　　　Hasleborrow,　　Clarke, of
bur. Dec. 28,　2nd husband　　Bradford　　　bap. July 20,　Chesterfield,
　1656,　　　Robert Watson　Hall from　　　1650,　　　Vintner,
Ferdinando　　　　of　　　his　　　　d. March 1,　bur. Feb. 5,
bap. May 13,　Wakefield,　　brother-in-law,　　1732　　　　1689
　1660,　　　　d. 1711　　John Wing-
bur. Oct. 27,　　　　　　field in
　1660　　　　　　　　1677
Robert　　　　　　　　bur. Jun. 7,
Margaret　　　　　　　1688
d. young

Benjamin Clarke of=Dorothy, dau. of　　Margaret=1. German Pole
Clarke Hall, Stanley,　Richard Stanley of　　　　　of Spinkhill
bap. Aug. 15, 1676　Arundel, Co. Sussex,　　　　2. Arthur Turner
bur. Nov. 11, 1703　d. June 9, 1729　　　　　　of Dewsbury

John Clarke of =Hannah, dau. of　　Ann Clarke,=Samuel Pegge,
Clarke Hall,　　William Hayford　heir to her　　F.S.A., D.D.,
Barrister-at-Law　of London,　　nephew Wing-　Rector of
bap. Jan. 12, 1701,　b. 1709.　　field Clarke　Whittington
d. Nov. 17, 1732　m. Nov. 20, 1726,　m. Ap. 13, 1732　b. Nov. 5, 1704.
　　　　　　　d. Dec. 26, 1753　d. 1746　　d. Feb. 14, 1796

Wingfield Clarke　　　　　　Samuel Pegge of=Martha, dau. of
of Clarke Hall,　　　　The Middle Temple,　　H. Bourne,
　b. 1728,　　　　　　F.S.A.,　　　　of Spittal, nr.
d. Mar. 18, 1750　　　settled at Clarke　　Chesterfield,
　　　　　　　　　Hall in 1758. Sold　　b. 1732
　　　　　　　　　it to Sir Michael　　mar. Feb. 9, 1759,
　　　　　　　　Pilkington in 1788.　　d. 1767
　　　　　　　　b. Feb. 21, 1733,
　　　　　　　　d. May 22, 1800

Sir Lyon Pilkington, of Stanley Hall on 14 hearths.
Gervase Hatfeild, of Hatfeild Hall on 10 hearths.
Mrs. Wingfield, of Bradford on   7 hearths.

Two years later, 1674, the same items are repeated
except that Mrs. Wingfield's contribution was on nine
hearths which was probably due to the present dining
room wing having being built with a fireplace upstairs
and down. This wing caused the south east projectory
gable to be pulled down for the later erection, as we
proved when repairing the oak panelling in the dining
room in 1914, finding two walled-up windows and the
cut-away brick and stonework of the original projection
of the Elizabethan E plan.

The Hearth Tax was repealed about 1689 when the
Window Tax was substituted by Sir Robert Walpole
to raise more money to fight the French under Louis
14th.   This tax continued until about 1843 when Sir
Robert Peel did away with it and gave us the Income
Tax and so the " last state of man was worse than the
first."

Mrs. Wingfield's daughter, Priscilla, married
Benjamin Clarke, of Hansworth, who bought Bradford
Hall from his brother-in-law, John Wingfield, in 1677
and came to live there.   He proceeded to alter the
Drawing Room by pulling down the old Tudor ceiling
of plain geometrical plaster panels with fleur-de-lys,
pomegranates and roses thereon, and substituting a
very ornate one showing the Indian corn plant as the
prevailing decoration and thus commemorating the
marriage of King Charles II with Catherine of Braganza,
daughter of the King of Portugal who brought the
Portugese colony of Bombay to the British Crown as
her dowry.   He also put up new oak panelling of the
late Stuart period as shown by the date 1680 on the
ceiling of the recess.

We found the remnants of the old plaster ceiling
left on the ground when a new floor was put down in
place of the decayed floor of 1680.   Benjamin also
changed the name of the house to Clarke Hall.   His

son, John Clarke, of the Middle Temple, married Hannah
Hayford, of London, and their only son, Wingfield
Clarke, died aged 22 leaving no family, and so the
estates went to Benjamin Clarke's daughter, Ann, who
had married the Rev. Samuel Pegge, F.S.A., LL.D., Rector
of Whittington in Derbyshire, in 1722.   He held various
fellowships at St. John's College, Cambridge, and was
Prebendary of Lichfield Cathedral, 1757-96, and of
Lincoln, 1772-96.   He died in 1796.   Their son, Samuel
Pegge, born 1733, was a barrister of the Middle Temple,
Groom to the King's Privy Chamber, Antiquary and
F.S.A.

Owing to their engagements elsewhere the Pegge's
did not reside much at Clarke Hall, but in 1759, they
let the house to Mr. Joseph Burrell, Master Clothier,
of Wakefield, who took a keen interest in town affairs
relating to the poor, employing some of them in his
mill in the preparation of cloth, which evidently came
up here to be dried and tentered, because one of the
nearby fields is known by the name of the " Tenter
Field " on the earliest map.

The Pegge's sold the Clarke Hall Estate to Sir
Michael Pilkington in 1788, in which year my great
grandfather, John Haldane, first rented a portion of the
Clarke Hall estate, later buying a field on which he built
a house, Ivy House, in which he continued to live.   He
eventually became tenant of the Clarke Hall land which
he farmed, but he let off the house to a Mr. Fenton
who for a time conducted a high-class school for young
boys.   In 1834 my grandfather, George Haldane, moved
into Clarke Hall, leaving his eldest son, Thomas, to
occupy Ivy House.   This was eventually sold to the
West Riding Asylum for a convalescent home for the
patients.   In 1855 my father, James H. Haldane, suc-
ceeded and carried on until 1902 when I became tenant;
and in 1914 I became the owner of the Clarke Hall
Estate.

After becoming owner I set about the restoration of the house, opening out 19 windows which had been walled-up to evade Window Tax. This brings to mind an old rhyme about the Tax " God made the light for man's good, Bobbie Walpole taxed it too—damn his blood!" I also stripped off the paint from oak panelled rooms and uncovered all the old Tudor and Stuart fireplaces which had been covered by Victorian period specimens.

On one of the diamond-shaped panes of a leaded light window is scratched " Redman Favell, 1712." He was a member of the old Normanton family of Favell born in 1694 and died in 1729. He married Ann, daughter of Richard Wordsworth, of Falthwaite, Cumberland, and great aunt of the poet, William Wordsworth.

Redman Favell was the eldest son of James Favell, of Normanton, who had married Elizabeth, daughter of Christopher Redman.

In Warburton's sketches (1712) contained in the Lansdowne collection at the British Museum, the house is shewn with a high-pitched gabled roof with dormer windows to the then garret chambers. Subsequently the house was entirely re-roofed with one of the hip roof type. Doing away with the garret chambers and raising the 1st storey bedrooms 3 ft. or so as shewn in the newer brickwork above the old windows.

A DESCRIPTION OF THE HOUSE

The original plan of the house was that of the Elizabethan E, showing three projections on the north side with its cobbled forecourt. The main entrance door is in the centre projection with its stone seal. On the south or garden side were two other projections to complete the E plan and the garden door with its fine ironwork and typical stonework surmounted with an old sundial.

One of these projections was evidently removed in 1674 when the present dining room wing was added because we found in carrying out repairs to the old panelling that on either side of the doorway was a broken-off brick wall with stone base of the same measurements as the Drawing Room projection and also a walled-up window at either side exactly similar to those existing in the other room.

It is quite possible that the existing stone plinth base of the house came from St. Swithun's Chantry on a part of the estate which was pulled down about the time this house was built.

The Hall occupies the whole of the centre or house-body of the building, with a fine flagged floor, which was intended to be covered with dry rushes at that period. The doors opening inwards are all four inches above floor level so as not to sweep up the rushes. The inner door of the north entrance is close to the ground because it would open to the screens which formerly would run from the kitchen to the cellar door. These no longer exist. But a very interesting feature is the strong oak bar which secures this inner door when closed. This slots into a hole in the wall when one opens the door, or pulls out and into a corresponding hole at the opposite side for securing the door against all intruders. The large open fireplace with its typical Tudor stone arch has a cast-iron fire plate or back showing the arms of King Charles I. The large iron fire dogs are still also in position, but are not now used for the large brands or logs of a few years ago. On the stonework of this fireplace are marks or grooves caused by sharpening arrows and sword blades.

The furniture is all of Elizabethan or Jacobean oak. One early oak cupboard with beautifully pierced panels for ventilation was found in the bed of the moat when it was run off in the early nineteenth century. After cleaning and drying it was brought back into the house and used in the Old Kitchen, until I had it touched up and restored to where I hoped was its original place in the hall, as mentioned in Brian (2) Bradford's will of 1558.

On one side of the hall was the Solar or the Drawing Room and on the opposite side was the kitchen and buttery. The hall was used for meals before the later dining room was erected.

The Drawing Room with its four windows is panelled in oak of late Stuart period and has a very fine plaster ceiling dated 1680. This room was evidently completely altered by John Clarke at that period when he came to live here and changed the name of the house. The stone mullioned windows with their seats are a nice feature of this room and also the quaint seventeenth-century Dutch tiles in the large fireplace.

This ceiling I have described earlier. On the opposite side of the hall and approached by a passage is the kitchen and buttery. This has now been altered to a breakfast room, the large stone archway of the kitchen being altered into an ingle-nook fireplace with two stone seats. The furnishing here is of old oak of the seventeenth century. Also is a nice collection of Scots' pistols, dirks and powder flasks. A new kitchen was built in 1929.

Also opening from the passage is the Dining Room wing, built in 1674 by Mrs. Wingfield for her son. This room is panelled in oak of that period and lighted by

three windows.   The large and projecting fireplace is
flanked by two deep recesses lighted by stone mullioned
windows.   A spring door in the oak panels of one recess
affords a means of escape from the hiding place
upstairs.   This room is furnished in Sheraton
mahogany furniture.

The upstairs rooms follow the same plan as those
downstairs and are approached from the hall by an
early oak newel staircase showing the fleur-de-lys
decoration in its pierced oak banisters.   The stairs
branch either way at the top.   To the left is the Great
Chamber with its beautifully figured Tudor panelling.
The use of this room in smaller houses of that period
was similar to that of the Long Gallery in the great
houses.   After the meal in the hall the ladies would
retire to the Drawing Room for a chat and the gentle-
men to the Great Chamber to talk news and business
before the ladies joined them later for cards and danc-
ing.   This room is lighted by four stone mullioned
windows fitted with original diamond panes.

Around the walls is a collection of armour and
weapons of fifteenth to eighteenth centuries including
a fine series of Scots broadswords and targes, and also
a collection of sixteenth and seventeenth-century
rapiers and eighteenth-century smallswords.   Above
the oak panelling is a series of helmets, pikes and
halberds with a number of red deer heads, etc.

There are also three suits of armour:—The suit of
an archer with chain mail shirt, etc., surmounted with
a helmet of the period of the Wars of the Roses, and
armed with a sword which was actually dug up on the
Battlefield of Wakefield (1460), a dagger and black bill
of that period; a threequarter suit of horseman's
armour of Charles I period, and also a cap-a-pie or full
suit of Elizabethan period armour from the Newstead
Abbey Collection, and said to have belonged to Sir
George Biron, an ancestor of Lord Byron, the poet.

Above the early basket grate fireplace and its
carved overmantel of quaint figures and carved panels
hang some half suits of armour and helmets of the Civil
War from Brancepeth Castle and Colonel Bright's suit
from Badsworth Hall, near Pontefract.   In this
chimney breast is the priest hole or cavalier's hiding
place which is entered by means of a sliding trap door
5 inches thick in the top of the long bow cupboard at
the top of the stairs.   A sliding panel in the carved
overmantel provides a food hatch. Two complete flagon
wine bottles were found therein when it was explored.
These were of the Civil War period and would have
served some Royalist fugitive as the Wingfields were
in favour of King Charles.   There is a small room
opening out of this room into the centre projection,
which was probably meant for an oratory.   The furniture is all of Elizabethan and Jacobean date.

From this room we enter the " Best Lodging " or
Guest Chamber with its three stone mullioned windows
and one later large one.   Note the very early wallpaper
and the open fireplace with the Dutch tiles and early
basket grate; also the very nice stone hearth, and the
carved oak fireplace.   The beautiful little plaster ceiling
in the projecting bay was rescued from a house which
was pulled down in Wakefield.   It shows vine leaves,
grapes and pomegranates' decoration.

Notice the very wide oak floor boards, 18 in. in dia-
meter.

From the stairs head to the right is a landing from
which through the very early oak party wall and beautifully carved doorway is the Second Lodging or Master's
Room with a fine pine eighteenth-century fireplace.

On the opposite side of this landing in the new wing
added in 1674 is the Oak Lodging with its perfect oak
panelling and a couple of Elizabethan four-post beds
with finely carved heads and canopies.

THE VISIT OF HER MAJESTY QUEEN MARY AND THE PRINCESS ROYAL

On August 31st, 1936, we were honoured by a visit from Queen Mary, Princess Royal and the Earl of Harewood, which had been arranged beforehand by His Lordship.

Her Majesty was very interested in the old house and its contents, showing a very great knowledge of antiques in general. After signing their autographs they promised to send me an old print of Harewood House to add to my collection of Old Yorkshire Houses, which they had seen in the Oak Lodging Room. This later came to hand with a beautiful Christmas Card from Princess Royal.

FROM SCOTLAND TO ENGLAND IN THE EIGHTEENTH CENTURY

A General Election took place in Scotland early in 1715, and this showed that the country as a whole was favourable to the Act of Union, uniting the two governments in one Parliament in London. John Haldane, the then Laird of Gleneagles, was returned as member for the County of Perthshire and was nicknamed " Union Jack " by the Jacobite Lairds around on account of voting in its favour.

Soon afterwards, the Jacobites broke out into revolt under the Earl of Mar and other adherents of the Stuart cause. These raised an army of 12,000 which they collected at Perth, while the Earl of Argyle assembled the Government troops at Stirling.

As the Jacobite army marched south they passed through the town of Auchterarder and over much of the Haldane estates of Gleneagles and Aberuthven, where they camped awhile and endeavoured to enlist recruits with very poor results, as their laird has advised them not to join. This caused the rebels to plunder and ill-treat the inhabitants.

After the Battle of Sherriffmuir, which both sides claimed to have won, the rebels again passed through the district and cruelly exacted much greater plunder About 700 of them camped in Gleneagles Park for a fortnight where they killed and consumed a great number of sheep, afterwards driving away 700 more, 60 head of cattle and all the horses belonging to the laird and his tenants. It was only because John Haldane's wife was a relative of the Earl of Mar and a supporter of the Jacobean cause that the mansion was not burnt down as were the houses and farm buildings of Auchterarder and Blackford with their stacks of corn and hay so as to impede the further advance of the Government troops.

In Auchterarder alone 142 houses were completely burnt down, also at Blackford, Aberuthven and Dalreoch which mainly belonged to the Haldanes. The families lost all their household plenishings and valuables, being turned out into a raging snowstorm with nothing but the clothes on their backs.   Many were killed or perished from exposure.

The Government promised to compensate the sufferers, but it was not until 1777, 62 years later, that they paid over to the then laird, George Haldane, £4,768 for division among the sufferers.   Many of these had died or left the district in search of more settled conditions and so got nothing.   We had gone south into Kirkcudbrightshire away from Jacobite feeling.

It was a severe and dour struggle to make headway without sufficient capital.   In the end my great-great-grandfather, James Haldane, who was born in 1740 and son of a survivor of the burning, decided to try his luck over the border in 1763, and so set off with a spade and a pack on his back.   There was no Welfare State in those days to help one through.

He came eventually into Yorkshire and got employment as a gardener at Haigh Hall, near Darton; he stayed there two years, during which he married Ann, daughter of Joseph Shaw, farmer, at Aketon Church.   Soon after this he moved into Wakefield where he rented the orchards and gardens called the Pear Trees which then extended from the Park Hills down to the river where now are the present railway sidings.   Afterwards he bought some land from the Clarke Hall estate and on it built a house where he was living in 1788, thus becoming a freeholder of Wakefield.   West Riding freeholders at that time had to record their votes at York and so he and his son, who were freeholders, used to walk to York, 29 miles on the first day, vote and see the sights of the city on the second day, then walk home on the third day.

They could have ridden free if they had sold their votes to either Whig or Tory, but that was not their principle.

Thrift, pride and independence were their characteristics.*

*"Haldanes of Gleneagles," by General Sir Aylmer Haldane, K.C.B. G.C.M.G., D.S.O., and "Annals of Auchterarder," by Reid.

The Chantry Chapel of St. Swithun was founded by John, the 7th Earl de Warenne about 1280 and stood alongside the old road leading from Lingwell Gate to the ford across the Calder at Kirkthorpe.   It stood midway between the present St. Swithun's Cottage and the junction of the road with the footpath leading from the Eastmoor to Stanley Ferry.

It was a substantial building of dressed stone 45 ft. long by 21 ft. wide. It was roofed with stone shingles as was determined when the site was excavated in 1905 by me. It was erected in order that a priest should say mass and hold divine service for the sick in time of plague, so that the rest of the parishioners might attend their parish church without fear of infection.   He endowed it with a rent charge of 40/- to be paid out of the revenues of his manor of Wakefield, with other lands of the yearly value of 50s. and 4d., the net stipend being £4 10s. 2d., and this sum continued to be paid until the dissolution of Chantry Chapels in 1537.

It had two bells, which when it was pulled down, were taken to the Chantry on the Bridge.

There were eight acres of meadow, three acres of arable land and a small cottage with a garden.   These were adjoining the park pale fence of the Old Park of Wakefield belonging to the Lords of the Manor.

EXTRACTS FROM THE COURT ROLLS OF THE MANOR OF WAKEFIELD
(Edward 1st, 1297-1307)

Court held at Wakefield on Friday before the Feast of St. Gregory, March 12th, 1307.

Richard, son of Patrick of St. Swithun v. Gilbert the Lister, of Birton, for trespass.

Court held at Wakefield on Friday, the Eve of the Nativity of St. John the Baptist, June 24th, 1307.

Adam, of Heley, fined 12d. for not having Gilbert the Lister, of Birton, to answer Richard, son of the Brother of St. Swithun.

Court held at Wakefield on Friday, the morrow of St. Bartholomew the Apostle—August 24th, 1307.

Richard, son of the Brother of St. Swithun, has licence to withdraw his complaint for trespass against Gilbert the Lister of Birton, because no attachment could be found upon the said Gilbert.

Court held at Wakefield on Friday, March 8th, 1308.

Henry, son of Symon Tyting v. Richard of Stanley for trespass. Pledge Symon Tyting. Benedict is attached by John of St. Swithun.

Court held at Wakefield on Friday in Easter Week, April 19th, 1308.

Robert del Spens wife 2d. Benedict of Stanleys wife 2d. John, brother of St. Swithun's wife, 2d., and William, the dyker's wife, 2d. These were fines for taking wood from the Old Park fence.

From the above it would appear that the chaplins of such remote chapels were allowed to marry.

Court held at Wakefield 1 Edward III (1327).

John de St. Swithun 3d. Thomas Gume 3d. and Naltham Hardre 3d. for taking palings from the Park Pale fence.

Court held at Wakefield, June 1st, 1324.

John de St. Swithun fined 6d. for vert.

Court held at Wakefield August 24th, 1324.

Thomas, son of German Filcok sues John de St. Swithun for secying cattle.

Court held at Wakefield on Friday, the Feast of St. Edmund, Bishop and Confessor, 18th Edward 2nd (1324).

Thomas, son of German Filcock, sues John de St. Swithun for taking 2 of her horses from a place called Colyhall in the town of Stanley (Colley Hall), etc., etc.

Court held at Wakefield on October 20th. Edward II (1328).

Thomas Gunne, John de St. Swithun and Thomas Adams wife fined 2d. each for dry wood.

Customary Court held at Wakefield. King Edward III (1327).

John de St. Swithun 3d, Thomas Gunne 3d. and William Hardi 2d., for palings.

WAKEFIELD MANOR COURT ROLLS
Saint Swithun's Chantry (The Dissolution)

To this court came the said Thomas Gargrave, Knight, and Thomas Darley, and took of the lord King one house, late a chapel of St. Swythen, near the old Park of Wakefield, and three closes of meadow lying about the said house, containing by estimation 8 acres of land, now or late in the tenure of Thomas Popplewell, and 3 acres of arable land in the occupation of Robert Burnell, and one small cottage with a croft to the same adjoining, in the tenure of the said Robert, and formerly belonging to the said chapel of St. Swythen near the Parke with their appurtenances in the graveship of Stanley or elsewhere within the lordship of Wakefield, to have and to hold the said house close, etc., to the said Thomas Gargrave and Thomas Darley, their heirs and assigns for ever, to the use and behalf of Thomas Westerman, clerk, for the term of his life, and after his

death to the use and behalf of John Cotton, gent, his
heirs and assigns for ever according to the custom of the
said Manor, and according to the form, effects and tenor
of a commission of the said lord King dated 2 April in
the 3rd year of his reign directed to John Tempest,
Knight, Chief Steward of the said court, and to Henry
Savile, armiger, under steward, there and in the rolls
of the said court enrolled as in the same rolls more fully
appears, which are granted to the said Thomas Gargrave and Thomas (Darley) to the use and behouf
aforesaid according to the custom of the said Manor,
etc.

YORKSHIRE

Chantry of St. Swithin under the Church of Wakefield Thomas Westerman Chaplain incumbent of the
Chantry.

Value of the same in Rent of lands and tenements in Stanley	2	8	8
Annuity received of the King paid by his Receiver at Wakefield yearly	2	0	0

                                               4 8 8

Full value

A deduction, viz.: A payment
to be made to the Bailiff
of the King in Stanley
yearly 1 6

Full value

Clear yearly value		4	7	2
1/10th part			8	8

From p. 79 Valor Ecclesiasticus 1538

First Battle of Wakefield was fought on Tuesday, December 30th, 1460.

The Duke of York as leader of the Yorkists arrived at his Castle of Sandal on Decmber 21st, where he collected a force of 5,000 men. At the same time the Lancastrians were assembled at Pontefract Castle 20,000 strong under the Earl of Northumberland and Lord Clifford.

On the morning of the battle a small foraging party was sent into the town for food supplies. On their return they were attacked by a strong force under Clifford coming down the Doncaster Road. Thus the fight continued as the Yorkists fought their way back towards the Castle. The Duke, thinking that Clifford's force was all he had to deal with, ordered all his men to leave the Castle and help the foraging party. Leaving the Castle unprotected they charged down the hill in a terrific snowstorm and drove the Lancastrians back towards the river where Porto Bello House now stands.

While this struggle was going on another force under the Earl of Wiltshire, which had approached the Castle by way of Carr Lane and Milnthorpe Lane, rushed in between the combatants and the Castle thus cutting off the Yorkists retreat to the Castle. They were outnumbered by 4 to 1 and a ruthless slaughter followed as no quarter was given. The Duke fought with great courage but was killed fighting with his back to a large willow tree.

The site of his death was marked up to living memory by a clump of willow trees at the junction of Manygates and Milnthorpe Lanes.

When the Duke's son became King Edward 4th he enclosed about a rood of land at the junction of these lanes with a fence, which he ordered to be maintained for ever and in this enclosure he erected a cross to his father's memory. This was destroyed by the Parliamentraians when they beseiged Sandal Castle.

When the present memorial was erected, this fenced plot was done away with to build the new Council School.

BATTLE OF WAKEFIELD SWORD

About 50 years ago in digging a trench for a drain an old sword was dug up which I secured and submitted to Sir Guy Laking, the King's Armourer, who described it as follows:—" The sword is of the fifteenth century and would probably be used as an auxiliary weapon for a crossbow man or archer because of its early rudimentary knuckle bow. The armourers mark — 3 ruondels, 2 and 1, with a mullel above, all within a pointed shield, occurs on both sides of the back edged blade. The cap-like pommel, straight quillon, knuckle guard are characteristic of the period. The total length of the sword is 33½ ins. and the blade 28¼ ins. x 1⅜ ins.

[Ex-Yorkshire Archaeological Society Journal XXII 128.]

This is the only known weapon from the Battlefield.

THE SECOND BATTLE OF WAKEFIELD

This account of the Battle I have taken from Dr. Walker's " History of Wakefield." I came across the field names of the " Cannonry," " Great Gun Croft " and the " Little Gun Croft " on old estate plans and showed them to him after I had identified the fields on the Enclosure Award Map kept at the Cathedral. I thought they must surely have got their names from either the Civil War proceedings or else the defences prepared by General Wade in readiness for the Jacobite Invasion of 1745.

Dr. Walker got his particulars from the House of Lords files of old newspapers of that period and so the full story came out.

The second Battle of Wakefield was fought on Whit Sunday, May 21st, 1643.

The town had been seized and garrisoned by the
Duke of Newcastle for King Charles and put under the
command of Colonel Goring.

On the previous day the Royalist officers had been
so sumptuously entertained by Lady Bolles at Heath Hall
that they were not in a very fit state for service when
the Parliamentarians attacked the town next day.
These left Howley Hall in Batley, the home of Lord
Savile, which had been garrisoned by Sir John Savile,
of Lupset, at 2 a.m. by way of Ardsley, the Lawns and
Outwood for Stanley.   Warning of their advance being
conveyed to Wakefield, 500 musketeers and some
Dragoons were sent to check their advance.   At day-
break the troops under Sir Charles Fairfax came up
Stanley Hill and to their surprise found companies of
musketeers lining the hedges in the field at the top of
the hill, which is now known as the Cannonry.   Also
at the junction of the road crossing Stanley Hall Park
with the main road was the Little Gun Croft.   The field
between the garden wall of Clarke Hall and the high
road is still called the Great Gun Croft.

Taking a number of prisoners and killing four men
they continued their advance to Wakefield, driving back
the musketeers lining the hedges along the Eastmoor
into the town.   The main assaults were at the head of
Warrengate and Northgate where the fight raged for
two hours.   At length the troops under Sir Thomas
Fairfax, in spite of volleys of great and small shot,
charged up to the barricades across Northgate, followed
by those under Colonel John Allured, of Hull, and
Colonel Bright, of Badsworth Hall.

Fairfax dashed down Northgate into the Bull Ring
which he found full of Royalist troops through whom
he charged, capturing two officers who surrendered to
him.   Finding himself without his own soldiers he
turned up the lane at the side of Radcliffe House and
the present Kiosk Cafe, followed by his prisoners. At the
top of this lane was a barricade defended by 15 or 16
foot soldiers, who, taking no notice of Fairfax, called

out to the two officer prisoners that they could not hold
out any longer. But the officers who had given their
parole to Fairfax, said not a word, and Fairfax, mounted
on his white horse, quickly cleared the barricade and
got back to his own men in Northgate to lead them to
the attack once more.

At the same time, Major-General Gifford's troops
forced the Warrengate Bar and attacked from that side.
The Royalists in the Bull Ring, from whom they cap-
tured some guns which they were able to turn upon
Colonel Lambton's three troops of horsemen as they
galloped up Westgate only to be put to flight by Fairfax's horsemen coming down Northgate.

By 9 a.m. all was over and great booty fell into the
hands of the Parliamentarians who retired to Leeds with
1,400 prisoners and much armament.

Sandal Castle was not surrendered until 1645, when
it was ordered to be slighted by blowing up with gun-
powder.

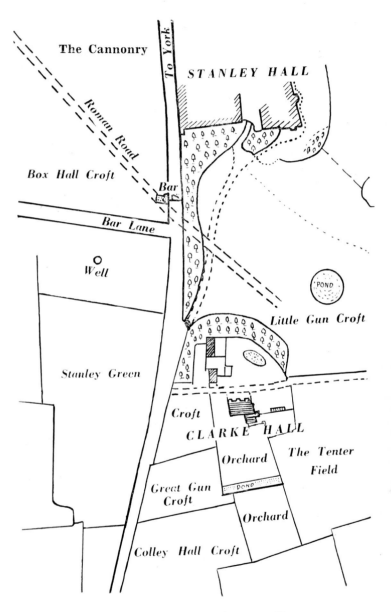

STANLEY GREEN AND THE ADJOINING HALLS

THE OLD TOLL BAR, STANLEY

STANLEY HALL IN 1712

CLARKE HALL FROM THE NORTH

Clarke Hall from the Garden

The Hall Fireplace

The Hall

THE MORNING ROOM

The Dining Room

DINING ROOM

THE DRAWING ROOM

THE DRAWING ROOM

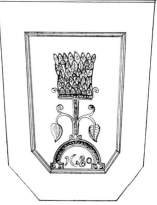

THE CEILING IN THE DRAWING ROOM

THE GREAT CHAMBER

THE GREAT CHAMBER

The Great Chamber

GREAT CHAMBER FIREPLACE

THE SLIDING PANEL IN THE GREAT CHAMBER

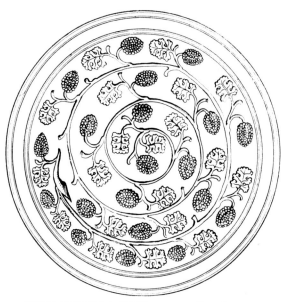

SMALL CEILING IN THE BAY OF THE BEST LODGING

FIREPLACE IN THE BEST LODGING ROOM

THE OAK LODGING ROOM

Dr. Samuel Pegge, D.D.

JOHN HALDANE OF GLENEAGLES, M.P. FOR PERTHSHIRE

GLENEAGLES HOUSE, PERTHSHIRE

IVY HOUSE

St. Swithun's Cottage

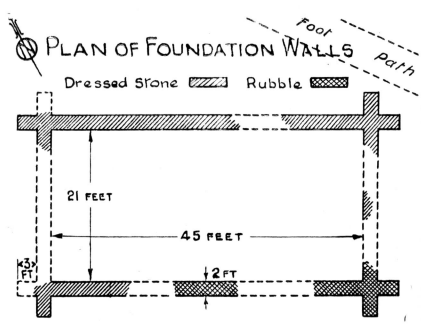

PLAN OF FOUNDATION WALLS

Dressed Stone [////] Rubble [XXXX]

Foot Path

21 FEET

45 FEET

3 FT

2 FT

Excavated and measured by H.C.Haldane Clarke Hall Stanley

PLAN OF ST. SWITHUN'S CHAPEL

St Swithins Chantry Wakefield

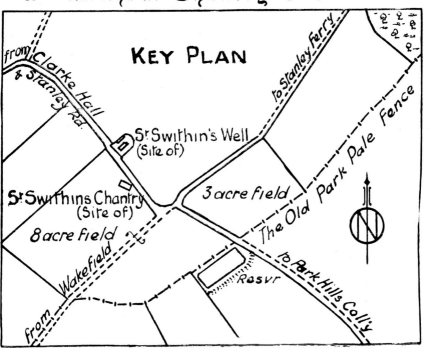

KEY PLAN

from Clarke Hall
& Stanley Rd.
to Stanley Ferry
St Swithin's Well (Site of)
St Swithins Chantry (Site of)
8 acre field
3 acre field
The Old Park Pale Fence
from Wakefield
Rosvr
to Park Hills Colly
N

A Relic from the Battlefield of Wakefield

THE AUTHOR HOLDING LITTLE JOHN'S BOW